A WEEK AT THE FAIR

A COUNTRY CELEBRATION

by Patricia Harrison Easton

Photographs by Herb Ferguson

The Millbrook Press ■ Brookfield, Connecticut

"Come on, Kristen," Dad says. "It's time to load the pigs."

I call Mom, my big sister Mandy, and my little brother Shane. Our county fair starts tomorrow. The week we've been planning all year has finally arrived. My family, the Buchleitners, has been going to the Washington County Fair forever. Even my grandparents went when they were kids. For the past four years, since I've been eight and old enough to join 4-H, I've been showing at the fair. This year I'm showing a market hog and my quarter horse.

Although "market hog" is the correct term, to me they are "the pigs." Today we have to take the pigs—mine and my friend Jen's—to the fairgrounds. Mandy's pig got sick early in the summer and didn't make weight. To show at the fair, market hogs have to weigh between 200 and 275 pounds.

Pigs can get very upset when you move them, so friends come to help us. At first the pigs won't leave their pen. Our dog Sparky thinks he's helping, but most of the time he's just in the way.

After a while I begin to wonder if we'll ever get these pigs onto the trailer. Finally, Dad grabs Jen's pig and hauls him out. The pig trots around the lawn in circles—squealing, panting, and shaking. He looks silly. Mom hoses him down to cool him off. If pigs get too excited they can get overheated and die.

Jen's pig calms down when my pig starts down the hill. We drive them toward the lower barn where Dad parked the trailer. Pigs are too stubborn to lead. We have to push them from behind, using boards to turn them. They surprise us and scramble right up the ramp onto the trailer.

Shane and I and our friend Matt pile into the back of the truck. We're ready to head to the fairgrounds, but we have to wait for Mandy, who takes a shower before she goes anywhere. The rest of us just go smelling like the pigs. We'll smell even worse by the time we get them settled in their pens.

At the fairgrounds Jen fusses over her pig. He's her first and she's named him Wilbur. I named my first pig, too, but these are market hogs and they're raised for meat. I learned it's too hard to sell a pig at the end of the fair if I've made a pet of it.

The next morning, Sunday, the fair officials weigh the pigs. My pig weighs in at 213 pounds, and Jen's at 232 pounds. "Good deal, Jen," I say. Jen and I won't have to compete against each other because the pigs are classed by weight.

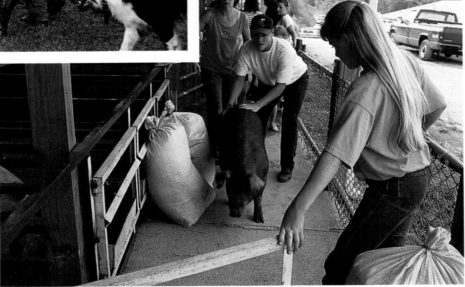

About noon it starts to rain. A neighbor says, "There's no surer way to end a dry spell than to open the fair." But the downpour doesn't last long. Later, as my friend Rendee and I walk by the draft horse barn, Phyllis, my 4-H club leader, calls to us. She asks us to carry flags in the opening ceremonies. We agree.

"All right!" Phyllis answers. "Now get me three other kids and meet me at the show tent."

We get Dawn, Megan, and my cousin Gina and go to the show tent like we promised. We each have to write a short biography about ourselves—how long we've been in 4-H and what our projects are—so the master of ceremonies can introduce us. Then we are each given a flag. I carry the Washington County Fair Flag. It keeps falling over my head. I push it off and the whole thing falls off the pole. "Dad!" I yell. He comes running and we get it tied back on just as they announce my name. My family laughs. As I walk on stage, I have to try hard not to laugh, too.

The fair is now officially open. We all smile. Even though we've already been here two days, our week has really just begun.

Monday morning we haul my colt and Jen's horse, Dusty, to the fairgrounds. Mom trains horses and gives riding lessons. She trained my colt and helps Jen with Dusty.

My colt is a two-year-old quarter horse gelding named Pretty Soxy Review. I call him Sox. After I get Sox settled in his stall, I'm free for the day. My friends and I watch some of the harness racing and the draft horse pull. The horse events are always my favorites.

Late in the afternoon Mom comes to the 4-H barn to get me. It's time to get my pig ready for his class tomorrow. Mom offers to wash him if I clean his stall. I think I get the best end of this deal. That pig has some nasty manure stains that take a lot of soaping and scrubbing.

When we get him back in his stall, it's time to shave him (not his whole body, just his ears, his tail, and his belly) to make him look neater. He's so tired from his bath that he plops down to sleep. I squeeze in next to him and get to work. When I'm done, he looks great—for a pig.

Tuesday morning we have to arrive before 7:30. The classes start at nine and my pig is in the second class, the medium lightweight class. He didn't get too dirty overnight, but he gets a quick bath anyway.

Soon I hear the announcer call, "Kristen Buchleitner to the show arena." I use my crop to drive my pig down the aisle and into the corridor to the arena. The first class is still showing when I enter the holding pen.

Sixteen pigs are in our class, which will be judged on the appearance of the pigs—how well they fit the breed standards for a market hog. But if I do a good job of showing my pig, then we'll be called back for the showmanship class. I hope my pig places well in this class, because that will raise his price on Saturday, but I also really want to be called back for showmanship.

I look at my family standing along the rail. They smile and I take a deep breath. The class starts. I work hard to keep my pig in front of the judge at all times. I am only supposed to touch my pig with the crop, not with my hand. It's hard, especially when the pig doesn't want to go where I want him to.

Two other pigs bump into each other and start to fight. The kids handling them step out of the way like they're supposed to, and two of the dads run in with a board and push it between the pigs. The kids then drive them away from each other. I move my pig away from both of them.

The judge motions for me to take my pig to one of the stalls at the far end of the arena. My pig has made the finals.

The judge takes a long time to make his final choice. When he chooses, he places my pig fourth, a good placing out of so many pigs. Then I hear my number called again. I've made the showmanship class!

I take my pig back to his pen and go to watch the show. Showmanship will be after all the other classes are finished. In showmanship my pig won't be judged—only I will be, on how well I show him. Jen and our friend Courtney have also qualified for junior showmanship. The seniors show first, then the intermediates, and the juniors last. Mandy stays down at the arena until after the senior class, and then she runs up to the barn. "This judge will keep turning her back on you," Mandy coaches. "You'll have to work hard to keep your pig in front of her."

"You know, Kristen," Mom says, "the judge may ask you some questions."

"What's your pig's best feature?" Dad asks.

I pretend to be thinking hard. "His tail," I say.

Dad just grins and shakes his head like he always does when I tease him. They call our class and Jen, Courtney, and I take our pigs to the ring.

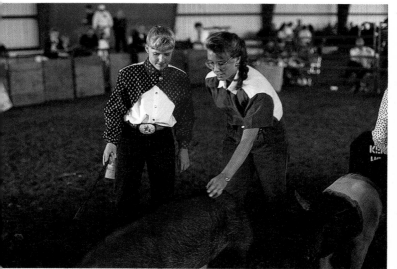

At first Courtney and I keep passing each other, back and forth in front of the judge. Some of the kids are having trouble with their pigs.

The judge walks over to me. "How much does your pig weigh?" she asks. I tell her. She scoops up a handful of dirt and, pretending to pat my pig, rubs the dirt onto his back. I take the brush from my pocket and brush my pig clean. I see her do the same to Courtney's pig. Like me, Courtney brushes her pig off.

Then the judge turns her back to us. Out of the corner of my eye I see Courtney turn her pig and drive it back in front of the judge. My pig is tired. I keep tapping the side of his head, but he just ignores me. He tries to go toward Jen's pig, which is rooting around in the dirt in a corner of the arena. Poor Jen. She's having more trouble than I am. I tap my pig harder and he turns, but I know Courtney has already made a couple of passes by the judge. The judge walks to the microphone.

"There were two outstanding showmen in this class," the judge says. "It was really hard to pick between them." Then she announces Courtney as the grand champion junior showman and me as the reserve. Back at the barn we proudly pose for pictures with our trophies.

I don't have any classes on Wednesday. In the morning we wander through the barn area. All kinds of animals compete at the fair and I love to see them.

It starts to rain late in the afternoon. We stand on the hill and watch puddles spread in the riding ring. The first day of the horse show is to-morrow. I sure don't want to ride an inexperienced colt like Sox in a sloppy ring. Luckily, by early evening the show committee cancels the show for tomorrow. They decide to hold all the classes on Friday.

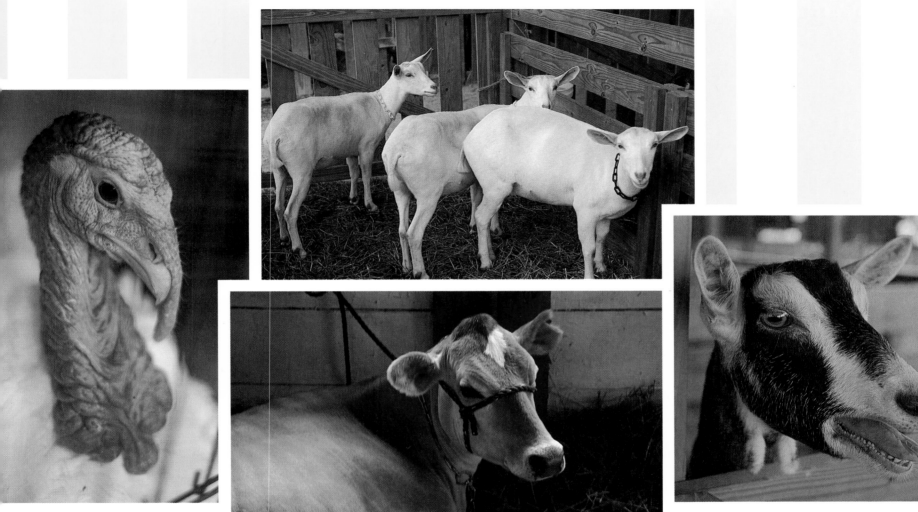

On Thursday it is still raining. This is a good day to head inside and look at the crafts and other exhibits. All the displays are great, but I like the wood carver best. He smiles at me but keeps on carving. He doesn't seem to mind being watched, so I stay awhile.

By late afternoon the sun comes out. I take care of my animals and leave the fairgrounds hoping that it doesn't rain again before morning.

It doesn't rain! We arrive early at the fairgrounds so I can groom Sox before the show. I brush him, shave off his whiskers, and clean out his hooves. I'm done with lots of time to spare.

Matt's sister Liz comes by with a puppy she bought from us. I take the puppy to see Sox. I think they seem happy to see each other, but Mandy says I'm imagining things.

Dad takes some of his sculptures down to display during the horse show. Dad's a blacksmith and makes sculptures out of horse shoes. They're really neat. Mom and I talked him into bringing them because that's what the fair is about—showing off what we've worked on all year.

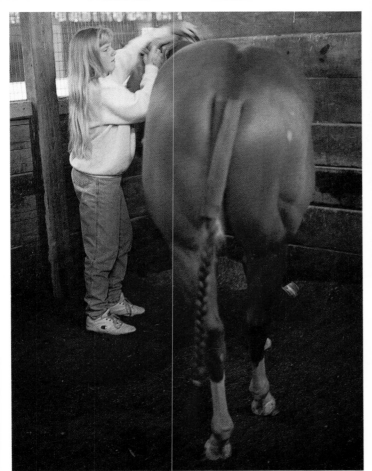

Soon the announcer calls the horses for the production classes. Now I have to hurry. Dad has parked our trailer by the ring, so I jump in to change clothes. Mom and Mandy adjust my tie and fix my hair.

The ring is still sloppy in the middle, so all the non-riding classes will be held on the concrete in front of the grandstand. Sox wins his production class, which is judged on his conformation—how he's built. We get a trophy and a blue ribbon.

I have to wait through the other production classes before I have showmanship at halter. I line up with the others and do my pattern—walk to the cone, trot to the judge, and set my horse up. Sox does everything fine but the set-up. At two he's still a baby, and he just doesn't understand why I want him to place his feet square. Still, he does a good job for such a young horse, and I'm proud of him. The judge pins us seventh out of fifteen.

Mom hurries to saddle Sox while I change into riding clothes. The western pleasure futurity is just two classes away. A pleasure horse is supposed to work slowly and easily, so I want to ride Sox a little to relax him.

We don't have much time to work before they call our class. Liz and I are the only ones entered in the futurity. The judge asks us to walk, trot, and canter and to back up along the rail. Sox makes a few mistakes, the kinds most two-year-olds make. I'm too busy to see how Liz is doing. We line up for the judge and she inspects our horses. I look at Liz and she makes a face. I guess she didn't have a very good ride. The announcer calls my name. Sox and I win the class. I look for Mom and give her a smile. She worked hard training him, and I know she's as proud as I am.

I have a long time until my next class, so I stand at ringside and watch my friends compete. Nobody stands around here for long with nothing to do. I get called to help set up the jumps for the hunter classes. Because the ring is so muddy, we use a wagon pulled by a team of Belgian draft horses, which tears up the ground less than the usual tractor.

About noon, my Aunt Debbie and Uncle Bill arrive from Ohio with my cousins. Gina and I take our little cousin Cylee to the petting zoo. Mom sends Shane to get me when it's time for my junior western pleasure class.

There are a lot of us in this class. Sox walks, trots, and canters just fine, but the other horses are more experienced and we don't place. I give him a pat anyway to let him know I don't mind. Sox and I will go on to the district show in the production class and the pleasure futurity. Jen and lots of my other friends have qualified, too. If we do well there, we will go to the state finals in October.

Friday night is concert night. This year John Anderson is performing. Mandy and I go, with our cousins and all our friends, to sit on the hill above the grandstand to listen.

On Saturday morning we arrive early to get the pigs ready for the market livestock sale. My pig has a big 29 stamped on his back to mark his sale order. I feel kind of sad. Dad says, "Selling our market animals is just one of the tough realities farmers live with, Kristen."

"I know," I answer. Besides, the money I make on my pig will help pay for show expenses for my horse.

I drive my pig into the ring, and the auctioneer begins to take bids. My pig sells to friends of ours, the Cowdens, for $1.20 a pound. I take the sale agreement over for Mrs. Cowden to sign and thank her for buying my pig.

For the rest of the afternoon we help with the sale. At dinner time we go to get something to eat. I find a booth that sells steak hoagies. They're good except for the green peppers, which I carefully pick out of my sandwich.

After dinner my cousin Cole, Jen, and I go to the midway for rides. Soon my cousin Justin finds us. I keep smelling cotton candy. I run and buy a bag for all of us to share. I like to save riding on the midway for the last night of the fair, after all the work is done. It's a treat I save for myself.

We wander by the side shows on our way back to the barn. All the kids always stay over on the last night. We have to talk Jen's parents into letting her stay with us. Since some of the mothers are staying, too, they agree.

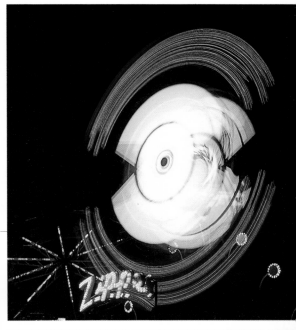

By midnight everyone is back at the 4-H horse barn. We've all put on warmer clothes and picked our sleeping spots.

"Go to sleep, Kristen," Matt says.

I know that half these kids have been planning pranks for this night all summer. "No way," I answer. "The first one to go to sleep gets it. Well, it won't be me. I don't feel sleepy tonight."

Even Jen has a can of shaving cream hidden in her sleeping bag. She is too impatient to wait for anyone to fall asleep. She squirts Ed, who squirts her back, and the shaving cream battle begins.

We laugh and talk until late and then everyone moves into the barn to sleep. I can't stay awake any longer.

Something tickling my cheek wakes me. They got me! There's lipstick all over my face. I go to the bathroom to wash my face and change my clothes. When I come back, I sit alone in front of the barn to watch the sun come up. I look out over the empty fairgrounds. No one is here but 4-H kids like me and a few of the county workers, friends to us, too, from our years of showing. One by one my friends come out to join me. I wonder how many of them feel like I do, that this is our special place. A few of the kids start to talk about plans for next year's fair.

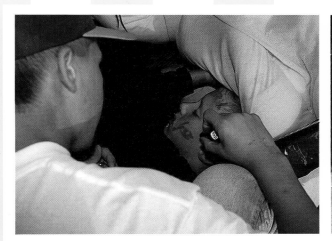

This year's fair is over. Some of us won. Some of us didn't. Some of us will go on to the state competition. Most of us won't. One thing's sure—we'll all be back next year.

Library of Congress Cataloging-in-Publication Data
Easton, Patricia Harrison
A week at the fair : a country celebration / by Patricia Harrison Easton;
photographs by Herb Ferguson.
p. cm.
Summary: The excitement of a county fair is experienced through the
eyes of a young girl who exhibits her horse and pig and joins her family
and friends in enjoying the fair's attractions.
ISBN 1-56294-527-0 (lib. bdg.) ISBN 1-56294-932-2 (trade)
1. Agricultural exhibitions—Juvenile literature. 2. Fairs—Juvenile literature.
[1. Agricultural exhibitions. 2. Fairs.] I. Ferguson, Herb, ill. II. Title.
S552.5.E27   1995
630'.74'73—dc 20   94-48120   CIP   AC

Published by The Millbrook Press, Inc.
2 Old New Milford Road
Brookfield, Connecticut 06804